TOWARD THE HANGING TREE

ALSO BY GINNY LOWE CONNORS

Barbarians in the Kitchen (poems, 2005)

Under the Porch (poetry chapbook, 2010)

The Unparalleled Beauty of a Crooked Line (poems, 2012)

TOWARD THE HANGING TREE

Poems of Salem Village

Ginny Lowe Connors

Yours in Poetry –
Ginny Lowe Con

Antrim House
Simsbury, Connecticut

Library of Congress Control Number: 2016943225

ISBN: 978-1-943826-10-0

First Edition, 2016

Printed & bound by Bookmobile

Book design by Rennie McQuilkin

Cover painting by Thomas S. Noble,
Witch Hill (The Salem Martyr)
1869, oil on canvas, 73 x 49 inches, object #1939.251
New York Historical Society

Author photograph by Brian Ambrose

Antrim House
860.217.0023
AntrimHouse@comcast.net
www.AntrimHouseBooks.com
21 Goodrich Road, Simsbury, CT 06070

for William, Lily, and Grayson:
May you give and receive compassion as you grow into your lives;
it is the beginning of wisdom.

ACKNOWLEDGMENTS

I am grateful to the PIPs (Partners in Poetry) who saw early drafts of many of these poems, and gave me valuable feedback: Sherri Bedingfield, Christine Beck, Tere Foley, Pat Hale, Joan Hofmann, Nancy Kerrigan, Julia Paul, and Elaine Zimmerman. I treasure your friendship and appreciate the many poetry-related adventures we have experienced together. Many thanks also to Patricia Smith, Michael Fisher, Jenneva Kayser, Angela La Voie, and Jon Riccio, who gave me encouragement, support, and fine suggestions along the way. Shannon McNeice gets a shout-out for her interest and ideas related to this project. Her judgment is impeccable and her kindness is unmatched. Liz Hanahan, a good friend as well as a descendant of one of the accused, gave me materials and perspectives I could have gotten nowhere else. Rennie McQuilkin's enthusiasm and fine editorial eye were invaluable to me as we worked to turn a manuscript into a book. Thank you, Rennie! Finally, I am thankful as always to have the unwavering support of my patient husband, Marty.

TABLE OF CONTENTS

SEPTEMBER-NOVEMBER, 1692

If only it were all so simple! If only there were evil people somewhere insidiously committing evil deeds, and it were necessary only to separate them from the rest of us and destroy them. But the line dividing good and evil cuts through the heart of every human being. And who is willing to destroy a piece of his own heart?

– Aleksandr Solzhenitsyn, *The Gulag Archipelago 1918-1956*

TOWARD THE HANGING TREE

January–February, 1692

Annie Putnam Visits the Parsonage

friend of Betty Parris and her cousin Abigail

A huddle of houses, barns and sheds.
A clutch of crows complaining on the weather.
My cloak held close, I step carefully along
a packed-down path through snow.

> There is Thomas Parris stacking wood, his face
> ruddy in the cold. He says nothing to me, just nods.
> Thinks he's too good for girls. Never mind—he'll be
> first to want the bread and jam my mother sends.

Inside the parsonage, near the hearth,
Betty and Abigail ignore their sewing, while little Susannah
plays with scraps meant for quilting. And there's Mary Walcott,
chattering away. Tituba scowls as she sweeps the snow

> I've tracked in, then goes about her business,
> out to the lean-to and back, carrying a kettle,
> keeping an eye on us, scolding and shaking her head.
> Mistress Parris is off tending the sick,

though she's thin as a stick herself, and the reverend
is gone somewhere. The air is sweeter when he's gone.
But the day is dim. It's drafty, and when the talking stops
we hear the wind. So we beg for a story of the olden times

> in old Carib. Tituba grunts and heaves herself down,
> stares for a minute at low flames in the hearth,
> and begins. *If you hear the sugar cane*
> *sing at night, rustle and moan—Monkey-man there.*

Monkey-man? Betty asks, a little shiver
in her voice. *Sure, child, Monkey-man, looks*
like a little old man with a monkey face.
He talk to the dead and fetch them sugar

> *so they get the strength to walk among the livin'.*
> The long winter day disappears as Tituba
> conjures spirits. Makes them dance from her tales
> right into our heads—until Mistress Parris enters,

wind slamming the door behind her, so we all jump.
Tituba stirs up some tea, Susannah is hushed,
and Mary and I make our ways home, where, like enough,
we'll be scolded for taking our own sweet time.

Abigail Williams Summons the Future

niece of Reverend Parris, living in the Parris household

Crack the egg, let the white
drop into a glass of water. Watch the shape
of the future, of our man's trade, his fortune
or his toil. Betty and Annie, Mary Walcott—and me.
We gather at the hearth, whispering,
wanting to know. Tituba nearby; she'll not tell.

A woman's fate depends on her man
so we wonder—what sort of husband
will we find—farmer, cooper, builder
of ships? The trade that makes the man
will take us into one sort of life
or another. A little magic will tell.

My turn. Candle and hearth—
shadows like creatures of the wood.
In the fireplace, a log breaks open.
Shower of sparks. We summon strange powers.
In the glass, the egg forms a plough? A nail?
No, a coffin!

We fall into screaming till Tituba turns sharp,
hushing us. *Throw that out!*
pointing her dark finger toward the door.
A wintery wind twists it in air,
a potion briefly flying.
We will not tell. Will not tell. Will not—

Betty Parris Hears Only No

daughter of the Reverend Parris

No running   no dancing   no wasting of time
No power   no nonsense   opinions   or rage
All of our stitches must march a straight line
No running   no dancing   no wasting of time
Stubbornness ugly   defiance a crime
I dream I've been captured   forced into a cage
No running   no dancing   no wasting of time
No power   no nonsense   opinions   or rage

Abigail Scares Her Cousin

Tituba cut off the head of a chicken
when Reverend Hale and his wife came to visit.
She'd in mind to make a nice stew.
Headless, the chicken flapped—almost flew—toward Betty.

It's bewitched! I told her. *And it follows you!*
'Twas all in fun. Betty opened her pink mouth wide,
let out an awful holler, and ran to hide
behind the shed. Where the ground has turned to mud.

After the bird was plucked and hacked and tossed
in the stew pot, I snatched one of the chicken feet,
whisked it away. Put it in a secret spot. The stew
seethed and bubbled, flavored with onions and herbs.

The Hales smacked their lips, and Uncle belched,
then tried to turn it to a cough. But Betty—
she picked at her food. Aunt 'Lisabeth said the child
had been peaked lately, nervous and pale. They sent

her to bed. Later I found the claw, waxy and hard,
right in the bedclothes with Betty. Told a tale
of how a witch had chosen her. *If a headless chicken
flaps all frenzied and follows you, watch out!*

Means an evil spirit's after your soul, I told her.
Said Tituba had whispered it to me, and it was true.
(I lied a little). *Seems it's attached itself to you,*
I warned my too-dull cousin. And so I had my fun.

But that night Betty woke us with her screams
and then she like to had a fit, shaking and thrashing,
talking wild stuff 'bout witches and chickens, how they
followed her. The family hovered, all sweet concern,

so I joined in the screaming too. Aunt gave Betty
bread pudding sweetened with honey, and after I hollered
'bout the witch, the devil, the horrid flapping thing—
I got some pudding too.

Thomas Parris In the Whirlwind

son of Reverend Parris

Again, my mother asks my father, *Where is the firewood promised to us?*

> My father mutters bitterly.
> So and so denying him his due.
> This and thus, the reasons.

> *Let us pray*, he says,
> *that their consciences will prick them soon, as well they ought,*
> *and they will give us what was promised.*

>> My sister Betty cries out. An evil
>> thing stings her. She slaps
>> at air, at herself, crying *Ow! ow! ow!*

My mother pales.

>> My cousin pinches herself and shouts
>> out garbled words. Hair in her face,
>> her body all bent over.

> My father's book thumps on the table, and he goes to her.

A buzzing like hornets all disturbed. I swivel
my head, one to the other. The air's hot and jumpy
like just before lightning.

>> Betty scuttles under the table,
>> a frightened dog. Her wits are gone.
Something prickles, back of my neck.

Betty, Betty, come out from there, my mother pleads, but Betty growls.
She flings herself against the floor.
There will be bruises.

Little Susannah starts in to crying.

Tituba
comes from the lean-to with her bucket
and scrubbing brush.
O girls, o girls. Shaking her head.

T'was her that done it! Betty shrieks.
And still at it!
Tituba, stop! Stop torturing me!
Then back to grunting and growling.

Susannah wails louder. I lift her up.

Her and Goody Good! my cousin screams.
And coming at me now—O, 'tis too terrible:
a bird with a human head! Don't bite me! No! I...I...
stop, I—
She flails, twisting her face this way and that.

My mother drags Betty into her arms,
where she thrashes. Growls. Tries to bite.

A tankard spills. A dish
leaps from the table.

My mother beseeches my father: *Samuel, for the love of God,
something must be done!*

                Loudly, my father starts in to pray.

         Tituba, head in her hands,
         frozen in the center of the room.

Outside, where it's begun to snow, wind howls.

      Inside, there's howling too.
            Everywhere such shrieking—demons
            are among us, though they're invisible to me.

Abigail Tries to Explain

My aunt's pearl brooch—it gleamed, and I meant
just to try it on. Tituba startled me! I hid it quick and then forgot.
When they found it with my things, my uncle thrashed me hard.
But wait! Let me—but he'd accept no argument.

I'm made to sweep the hearth, and I must learn to spin,
read from the Bible, pray for forgiveness and think
about sin. This is not who I am. I want to ride a horse unsaddled,
dance in the moonlight, try out forbidden things.

I'm scared. A spirit glared at me last night; its eyes were red.
A wilderness wrestles in my head. Nobody knows what I see.
Invisible spirits torture me. I'm pinched, I'm pained.
I'm twisted, grieved, blinded by a cloak of dread.

Tituba Makes a Witch Cake

a slave serving the Parris family

Abigail—that child! Poked a log from the fire, kicked it
'round the room till the house fill up with smoke.
Fire! Fire! Flames grow higher! she shouted out
and Betty fell down moaning,
began to choke.

Next day's news—a neighbor's house had burned!
And a baby-child died. The reverend's white face
went pale and paler. Then Abigail said
The devil's mistress is about! Came
to me, and Betty too.

What to do? Rye meal and hot piss, baked in ashes—
that make a witch cake. A cake to draw the witch
from hiding. Goody Sibley said to make that cake.
And she a Christian woman.
Told me *Try it!* So I did.

I would never hurt those children. I love those children.
Was the devil's own familiars tortured them.
Abby claimed it to be true, and Betty too.
The witch cake were never *my* idea,
but *I'm* the one dragged away.

Rye meal and hot piss, baked in ashes—I made a witch cake.
Abigail spun around and shouted, *Tituba! Tituba!*
Twists my neck! And then she fell.
The reverend caned me hard,
demanded me to tell

about the witchcraft I'd been doing. But all I could say
was *I never hurt those children. I love those children!*
Think they'd listen to me? Dragged me away
and searched me for witch marks
though I got not a one.

Reverend Samuel Parris, Besieged

Pastor of Salem Village; the witch-hunt began in his home, the parsonage.

Enemies conspire against me. Enemies without and within
my own household. My faith, still strong, seems thin
protection. Amongst us, the Devil has been raised.
My wife is ill; my girls fall into fits. For days
on end they contort themselves, pricked with invisible pins.

And neighbors eye us hard, thinking Satan has moved in.
Tituba baked the witch cake. It was her sin
that brought this on. I strike her, not *her*, nay—
I beat at her witchcraft, her wickedness. I'd lay
my hands 'round the throat of the Devil, could I find him.

But now the evil spreads. Others join the din
of writhing girls: Young Ann, Elizabeth, Mercy and Mary say
they're pinched, they're jabbed, their sight falls away.
Dark Forces press close, and enemies conspire against me.
Cursed be such sinners, and all my enemies, without and within.

Reverend John Hale Recalls a Witch

a prominent minister in the nearby town of Beverly, consulted by
Reverend Parris

Beware. I lived near a witch when I was a child.
Margaret Jones—she had an evil eye, but never would confess.
A neighbor argued with her once, and then his cows went wild.
Take care. I lived near a witch when I was a child.
Her touch caused deafness, rash, or piles.
Boy threw snowballs at her once, then suffered weeks of fever
    and distress.
A sad affair. I lived near a witch when I was a child.
She had an evil eye, but never would confess.

Beware! The magistrates exclaimed, *The devil's mischief is afoot*
and we must stop it.
I knew her and was scared. But she was put away. She could
have wreaked such havoc. Witches answer to the devil,
    oh he of cloven foot.
The air turned brassy when she hanged. A tempest tore
    through Connecticut
lifting roofs, spreading fires, covering fields with soot.
A sad affair. Now in Salem Village, another storm's afoot.
And we must stop it.

Goody Abbot Consults Goody Taber, Who Warns Goody Wright

local women

It was the rain that hissed. Grease spattered on the hearth.
Or was it the devil's kiss, evil whispering in your ear?
       Even the glance of a witch can burn;

I mean your very flesh can seethe and blister.
Beware the devil's kiss, evil whispering in your ear.
       An omen: cream that sours in the churn.

Is it prayers the old woman mutters, or maledictions
that sting your flesh, make it blister?
       Could be just the rain that hissed,

or an old woman's prayers. But a witch's maledictions
will sicken your stock, turn your crops black.
       Even the glance of a witch can burn.

And when your healthy babe, sweet dumpling, is stricken
look sharp! It could have been a witch.
       You won't always know the devil's kin.

A wart, a cyst, a sty may be a witch's mark.
You won't always know a witch. Her glance can burn.
       She mutters maledictions.

Look sharp! Tiny tag on the skin—a witch's teat.
Dark magic is a yellow cat, a big black dog, a path
       beset with toads. A wart, a sty—witch's teat.

Beware the yellow cat, a path beset with toads.
A sound like the rattling of stones in the throat
        of a yellow bird. It foretells a witch!

Beware of poppets, stuck with pins.
Beware your neighbor, beware your sins. When the devil
        sidles up to you, he grins.

And watch for the child who shakes,
who moans, crouches helpless in the corner,
        contorting her limbs.

A child who's fevered, one with fits. A girl who moans.
A sound like the rattling of stones.
        You won't always know a witch.

Mary Warren's Secret

Mary was the young servant of John and Elizabeth Proctor.
Thorndike was a son of John Proctor from a previous marriage.

Taller than his father, and strong. He comes
and goes. Behind the barn, he kissed me,
Thorndike Proctor did, and touched my cheek
and more. His chin was bristled, a smudge
of dirt marked his brow. His breath came quick
and smelled of onion. Then I heard the mistress
calling me—a raven's shriek's more tuneful—
and we tore ourselves apart.
Wool to be carded, flax to be spun.
The porridge to stir, a child crying in a corner.

Within my skirts I've pinned a packet
of rosemary, lavender, sage, crushed fine
with a handful of parsley and a pinch of thyme.
Goody Osborne gave it to me. An odd sort of woman,
but she knows medicinals, herbs and charms.
A love charm? It might be that. Or just something
to freshen my woolens. But Thorndike? Mostly
he stays away. Though he sat at the table today.

His calloused hands gripping a cup
made me turn from him, a knot in my throat—
the air's too close in here. And then the sharp
voice of the mistress slicing into me. Chores
to be done and nothing ever
satisfies that woman. Wool to be carded,
flax to be spun. *Idle hands are the devil's*
workshop, she scolds, while leaving

the drudgery to me. The devil's dark ways—
who's more likely to fall under that spell
than her, I'd like to know?

I keep busy. Set my mouth to closed
though my eyes are always open,
following Thorndike when he's near.
He gives me one look, then shakes his head, turns
to go. Before I ever really had him, I'm losing him,
I know it. What stays with me
are all the thoughts I should not think,
whiff of onion, my secret wound.

Annie Resists

Deceitful beggar, hag, and witch!
Sarah Good is no ways good.
I'm scared to look on her; I shake, I'm sick.
Nights, her shadow rides a stick!

       Oh *help!* She twists my neck, she pulls my tongue!
       There's needles in my palm—look what she's done.
       And no I won't, I won't, I *won't* write my name
       in the devil's book. Though she insists I must.

Even her daughter, small as she is, turns on me
an evil look. Bites me—ow!—and ow!
and pinches me again—her spectre's strong
and hateful. *Stop!*

       Last night I woke from a fearful dream
       or was it that old witch? Again I'd refused
       to sign the Devil's book, though she thrust
       it toward me, promising gifts. My shouts

brought Mother running. She found me bruised,
my nightclothes torn, and there on the floor
the same clay pipe that Goody Good
is known to smoke. That beggar, hag—that witch!

March–May, 1692

Betty Is Sent Away

Betty was sent to stay with relatives: the Seward family in Salem Town.

We stirred up the devil with our fortune-telling game. That's all it took.
A darkness entered me. A hurt. I flung myself around at prayers.
My skirts were brambled with those seeds they call the devil's hook
after I chased the Fosters' goat. Next day I threw the Good Book.
They will not have me here no more. I guess I wear the devil's look.
My mother even tells me, *Go.* I see my father's stone-like stare.
A darkness entered me. A thrill. I flung myself around at prayers.
We stirred up the devil with our fortune-telling game. That's all it took.

Mary Knows

I know about sin.
Invisible, but it's there, like the wind
that tries to get inside your skin
or like the dream as real
as a pricker bush pulling at your dress,
as sure as a rolling pin—
but the dream lives inside you,
invisible to others. That's sin.
It's heavy, like water in buckets
I carry back from the well,
trying not to spill. My mother died
of it and my little sister
took quite ill.

Sin is musty, like rotten straw
stuffed in a mattress
or it's restless—the secret
you've promised not to tell.
It's the thin odor of metal
in the drop of blood, dark red,
that serves you right
when you're careless with the needle
as you mend. It pricks like a pin.
It smells like a toothache
or like a charred broom
with its history of fires
that wish to spread.

William Good Renounces His Wife

husband of Sarah Good

She married me, was good to me for thirty-three days—and then started in to complaining. She took it hard when I could not pay her debts. More than once she's scratched my face, left me bleeding and bewildered—I think I loved her back before, but no more. Sarah's hands, once soft and kind, are claws. I try to keep my distance. We go about begging for shelter or work, for mercy, though it was not like this before. I could plow a field straight, could help raise a barn; I could drink more ale than most, and still manage. She talks to rats, she mutters curses, and goes about ragged and filthy. Insects in her hair. Summer evenings she feeds our daughter frogs roasted over fires she starts with a twirl of her fingers—it's not right to eat frogs—they swim in slime and their throats bellow out something awful when they croak and chant into an evening's gloom. Fall days Sarah gives the child sour apples, wormy and waspy, and what can I do—I've lost my home and hardly a one will hire me for a decent day of work. I think she's cursed me. I tell you now, the devil's mark is on her shoulder, nearly blue, looks like a bite, and there's witches teats under her arm—where did they come from I asked her once but she just hissed at me and stayed away for a fortnight or more. And just when I start into hating her, she draws me close and breathes out spells till I can't help myself—I feel for her, the way a man feels something for his wife, but soon she drops away from me like I'm a worm landed on her supper. You can't look in her eyes more than one second or your face will burn. Oh, the one I married was carried away; this creature's taken her place.

I know not what will become of her or me or the child whose hair is knotted like a knocked-down sparrows' nest for—a girl child, what should I do for her? I was lonely once, but now it's worse—I'm fearful. Surely she's tight with the devil. I've married a witch. My eyes burn even as I say it. My life blisters in her presence.

Thomas Wonders

My father paces, his hair all a-touseled, a glint
in his eye. In Falmouth and Casco
and such like places, Indians attack. But here
it is neighbors we fear.

For when the devil tempts them, some do give in.
My father drums his fingers, stomps off
to meetings, whispers in corners with other men.
My father and the magistrates—we're told
to put our faith in them. I try.

The devil's rage is terrible, my father says,
and it may be the witch cake lured it out.
Or other magics or even just our sinful
thoughts. I sin sometimes. I doubt.
But do not tell my father this.

Goody Osborne's held in jail. An old,
half-witted woman. Goody Good is with her,
and her little girl too. Good's a likely witch,
the way she drags around in dirty clothes,
begging and muttering. But the little one—

they had to make special chains for her,
her wrists are so slender. I look at our own
Susannah, sorting through a lapful of acorns
as if they were jewels. Imagine her chained
in some dark jail. It's hard to fathom.

Sarah Osborne Admits a Few Small Sins

one of the first to be accused; thought to be mentally unstable

Dank prison, mildew and rot. Blood and snot.
Things crawl on me. It's cold. I'm coughing, but—
Confess to things I never done? By the rat's tail, I'll not!

    Broken Twigs. Sour Figs. Shiny eggs of earwigs.

Quarreled, uh huh, with them holy-moly Putnams,
broke all the yellow blossoms from the plot
Ann tended to so carefully. And then I fed 'em to the pigs.

    Mustard grass. Striped ass. Sharp scent of sassaphras.

Woke to an owl calling my name. Unlucky light
spilt over my face. Moonlight slipped from its brassy pot.
Dawn—bloody feathers on the stoop. Lick of fright.

    Wooly coot. Holler, hoot. Broke-off tail of speckled newt.

Looked crossways at a horse once to make it spook.
Oh, I done things. But confess to a witch's lot? I'll not!
Dank prison—here I crouch. Shiver, cough, and puke.

Tituba Confesses

At first I say, *I have done nothing wrong. I never see no devil.*
But people think, If anybody be a witch, Tituba must be.
The men frown hard at me; the girls they twitch,
stick out tongues, fall to the floor and shout.
Every one of 'em got more power than me.
'Bout now, I wish I *was* a witch.

I say, *I have done nothing wrong. I never see no devil*—
but they hang the ones that don't confess.
I not a bad woman. I just want to live.
So I take a breath and say
I saw a thing like a man.

The men frown hard at me; the girls forget their act.
The man-thing want me to hurt the children,
but I say no. I take a breath and say,
It came in the night, the hairy man.
The judges—they want more.

We rid a stick to Annie Putnam's house to pinch that girl.
Goody Good and Goody Osborne was there.
They had a knife. If harm came
to these children, I say
I'm sorry for it.

People think, If anybody be a witch, Tituba must be.
I know they hang the ones that don't confess.
I not a bad woman. I just want to live.
If harm came to these children,
I say, *I'm sorry for it.*

Mercy Lewis Sees the Signs

a servant girl for the Putnam family, and one of the chief accusers

Mercy, what say you about witches?
What has the talk been, and what do you know?

Last week Jeremiah Bray's cow jumped four feet in the air.
Anne Russell near fell into the fire; pushed by an enchanted chair.
A broom was lodged high in the Parris's apple tree. Who put it there?

How strange! Unnatural—have there been other signs?
Mercy, what else have you heard?

Richard Allen's horse, the chestnut mare that's slow and old
reared up, foamed at the mouth, and galloped down the road.
Richard says whatever scared the horse had eyes that glowed.

Mercy, oh Mercy, is the devil about?
Can we keep such evil away if we pray, if we're devout?

White cat with a man's face hurled itself at John Indian. He'll tell you more
if you ask. The Putnams' crockery flies from the shelf, shatters on the floor.
Last evening a bucket of half-froze toads appeared at their back door.

Oh Mercy, those are signs, are they not?
Three have been accused. Are there others?

After that little beggar Dorcas laughed and stuck out
her tongue, my friend seized and choked. And without doubt
Goody Corey is a witch. A yellow bird's been following her about.

Bridget Bishop Protests

a sharp-tongued woman who quickly fell under suspicion

Because they do not like the way I dress,
      my red bodice with its loops of colored thread.
Because folk drink cider ale and play shovel board
      in my tavern, even on the Sabbath, and I allow it.
Because I fought with my second husband and do so
      with my third, the old rogue
I should bow and scrape when he's unkind?

They believe I torture the Lewis girl, the Williams girl,
      and Anne Putnam's simpering daughter.
      Stick them with pins and other such nonsense.
Believe my apparition laid down on Samuel Gray at night,
      tried to choke him.
      This man who lingers at the tavern, making eyes,
      when his wife would have him home.

They look at me and all but lick their lips, hell-bound
on hanging me. I ask you, who is it does the devil's work?

June–August, 1692

Thomas Holds On

Sharp and black and shiny,
chiseled stone, the arrow heads I find
are my amulets. They're not godly at all,
I know that. But they protect me.

Gathered in a leather pouch I found hanging
on a bush near the swamp,
a bush with berries red as poison.
My arrow heads, my secret cache.

To shake stone wedges into my palm,
touch their cool, chipped surfaces
is to feel their dreams,
dreams of the hundred hunts of savages

who knew these woods. They shot
at targets real and fleshy, muscular—
not like invisible enemies
the girls fight off, cry out against,

the ones that have turned my father
into a burning man. His eyes glow
in a face that twitches with fury.
When his jaw unlatches, thunder

falls among us. Who has he become?
What is this place we've landed in?
Like sickening vapors, spectres
drift into a room, turn us against one another.

Goody Taber Tells Goody Abbot and Goody Wright What She Saw

Goody Howe was on the stand. Accused but denying it all.
And I saw it: children jabbed with needles. A girl blinded
     by the woman's piercing look. A witch indeed!

Goody Howe? I never would have thought it!
Oh yes. Drinks a tea boiled from beetles. Well, *I* heard
     the Putnams writ a complaint on her. Putnams and Howes—

they never was friendly. Perhaps, but I was there and saw it: a child
falling down, another bleeding. The Williams girl let out
     a piercing shout. *Her Demon spits at me! Says Howe will hurt*

a woman's legs! And right then Goody Putnam screamed. Her legs rose
in the air, quite against her will. She fell back, sobbing and shaking.
     Next, Mary Walcott began to twist and jerk.

And it was told a neighbor's cow birthed a calf that had two heads.
This was after Goody Howe was angered at those folk.
     The falling, the screaming, a calf with two heads—

Goody Howe was found out. Led away, and rightly so.
She drinks a tea boiled from beetles. Now four others are accused.
     The hearing's set for Tuesday. Will you go?

Not I. My duty is at home. And…I'm scared to go.
Get close to a witch, or a child afflicted, and before you know,
     they'll accuse *you* of spells! Say you made their hog leap up

or you rode a stick at night, or sent the pox to sicken
someone's child. Why, any of us could be accused!
          Oh, Lydia, you're no witch! Nothing could be said

against you. Well, maybe not—but I'm confused.
They say the Devil can take the form of anyone, a person pure
          and guileless. And others may believe in the delusion.

I know. I feel unsettled too. Satan may be near us even now,
or his familiars that answer to his call. They're in the air.
          They're everywhere. They look for weakness, a little sin—

and jump right in. But why *here*? I've heard a coven gathers
in the reverend's pasture when the moon is full. And dance
          there half-naked, drink blood, court the Devil.

Remember, Parris said Satan goes where he's most hated
and tries to wrestle out a victory. Yet where the Devil goes,
          God's never far behind. So we must roust the witches out

and fast and pray. Then evil will give up, and goodness stay.
I pray you are right and that our troubles end. But when they haul
          our neighbors in for judgment, I'll stay away.

Elizabeth Proctor Talks Back

Elizabeth Proctor was the matron of a prosperous family. Mercy Lewis was one of the girls who accused her of witchcraft.

They say

I am darkness in a woman's simple dress.
My spectre—and my husband's too
torment innocent girls, scratch them, tear at their bowels.
My touch burns.

           I say

           It is their words that burn,
           their spite that stings,
           their pointing fingers that condemn
           good souls to a dark cell
           or to the hanging tree.

They see me flap up to the rafters and perch there,
a clawed creature spewing venomous spells
so girls twist their limbs and shriek
or fall down, insensible.

           These accusations pierce me
           the way a terrible, funneling storm
           I once lived through
           drove a thin piece of straw
           deep into the trunk of an oak.

           It quivered there afterward. Frail thing
           or unyielding arrow, we knew not which.

Within me, a child kicks.
To be born, if God allows, into a world

where Mercy is not
the idea of goodness
but a girl with an adder's tongue.

Tituba In Prison

That beggar woman with her two children.
Lil raggedy girl rocking back and forth,
hardly talks. Child's mind spins
in her head like a top, won't
settle, won't stop.
Her spirit's torn
itself away.

And the woman has a baby, a puny thing,
fussing at the breast. Two blankets sent
to wrap the wee one in. The men—
they call that kindness.
Baby's weak, mewls
just a little, waves
a useless fist.

Never had no sweet babies of my own. No boy
nor girl to call me Mama, none to watch
grow strong and bright, or suffer
for the sin of being dark.
Other people's children
the ones I've cared for.
They sent me here.

Annie, Unable to Sleep

The voices wake me up. The floor tilts—they growl
my name. They can sound like the mewling of cats
or the scratching of mice in the walls. They screech
like animals attacked—they threaten me; they howl.

    They say I'm worthless! Should be dead! The shapes
    of demons and witches, spiraled into smoke
    encircle me. They pinch and pull and bite. They're big as trees,
    whiskered like rats. Ghastly neighbors, cloaked and draped.

Sometimes I break in two. One of me screams and fights,
strikes out, struggles, groans and shakes. The other
stands off in a corner, silently watching it all. My mind
is a tribe of magpies, chattering. Then, still as ice.

Joseph Leech Does His Duty

the hangman

Not a job I ever set out to do
but as assistant sheriff
I do what Corwin tells me to.
Bridget Bishop was the first.
A stubborn woman, she wouldn't admit
to witchcraft, even at the end,
when it might've helped her some.
Most likely she was a liar. She showed
no shame for all her wicked ways,
but what if—

No matter. I had to guide her
up the ladder. Her legs was shaking. She clung hard
to every rung and had to be prodded some
to go on up. The rain was done,
the heat was out. Sweat—it made my shirt stick,
and trickled down my sides. Gnats swarmed us so,
I wished I could swat 'em away, but my hands
held the ladder and urged the witch woman on.
Bridget Bishop. Truth is she smelled. Her neck
was grimy; her hair hung in oily clumps. A smell
of musk, of fear, sour and heady all at once
came roiling toward me.

One rung at a time we went up. Crowd below us
shouted things, horses side-stepped

and snorted. A boy threw a rock that went
skittering past the witch's cheek.
Oh God, Oh God, she muttered,
and then she retched. Little gold specks
floated before my eyes and sparked—
I wondered if it was her doing.
Some sort of last-minute spell.
How shameful if I fell! *I'm no witch*
she told me. *My death will be
a darkness on your soul.* But I
had my duty and I did it.

They passed the black hood up to me
which I placed around her head
while she protested, twisting around,
staring at me with huge gray eyes in a face
so pale she might've already been dead.

I reached for the noose that hung
from a sturdy branch. Arranged it
around her neck, almost tenderly.
These would be her last moments.
With another length of rope
I tied her hands behind her back,
the hemp stiff and splintery.

What makes someone a witch? For years
she lived among us and we didn't know.
She was crying harder now,
and between the sobs sucking in breaths
like someone about to drown.

Shaking some. A minute passed,
an hour, or a day. A feeling sneaked
into me: glad it was not *me* with a noose
around my neck. A final prayer said.
Then Corwin called up the command.
I sucked in some wind and I did it,
just did it—pushed her from the ladder.

A roar from below. The ladder shook.
Carefully I climbed down while she swung
and twisted in the air. Kicked her feet.
A field of sparks before my eyes.
A cold sweat. Had to rush toward the bushes
for this was my first hanging, and I was weak.

Rebecca Nurse At Home

70 years old and bed-ridden, Rebecca was known to be very pious.

Martha, my youngest daughter, expects her third child.
I'd embroider some gowns for the baby, and a little cap.
I'd knit a blanket of softest wool. But
my fingers are stiff, knuckles swollen, and my eyes—

they've lost their sharpness. I'm not so useful anymore.
Never mind, Martha says. *Watch Polly for me. Listen to her read
from the Scriptures.* Polly's a bright child, a good girl.
Knows all her letters and puts the words together well.

True, sometimes she mumbles. I tell her to speak up.
Martha comes in, shakes her head, says, *Your shoes ring,
now what are you fearing?* At length I learn
what she meant to say. *You're losing your hearing.*

But I hear the tales our neighbors tell. Mutterings
of witchcraft. A pack of girls gone screaming. The talk
is dark magic, strange fevers, poppets and pins.
Young girls afflicted. My heart goes out to them.

Rebecca's Confusion

What is that screaming? Why, Goody Putnam,
who hurts you so? Young Annie, is that you? And Mary Walcott?
Please, no, what do I know of witches?
The questions confuse me; my hearing is poor.

Ann Putnam claims what? I visited her
at dawn, in my night clothes, with a hooked rug that I designed?
Oh, you mean *a book I tried to make her to sign?*
The devil's book! But I have been sick in bed, how could—

Rebecca Imprisoned

Just a shawl against the chill. Women in chains—
their groans, their stink. How does one breathe
in this place? It's dark, and darkness fills me.
Feels like I'm under water. How did I come to this?

I know nothing of witches. I've loved my husband,
my children, and God. If I could wrap myself in a quilt...
if I could sip some steaming tea...the ache in my hips,
my chest.
And I am cold. The others here—how have they borne it?

Is that...a child? Small moaning creature,
rags and matted hair. Sarah Good's child?
Who would do this to a child?
To any living creature? Dorcas, her name is.

She cries and rattles chains. A dark shape—
Tituba—why that's the reverend's slave—speaks to the child.
Hush she says, and something about a story.
But neither Tituba nor I nor God can comfort her.

Israel Porter Observes

a wealthy and respected citizen

I've stood in the back of the meeting house
during the hearings, in the close stale air
among the coughs and the shuffling,
amid the smells of unwashed hair,
the sour musk of sweat and fear. And girls
who are nothing, who are nobody,
who are not yet women, who know nothing,
fidget on the front bench, whispering.
Martyrs or impostors, it's hard to say,
but they seem a bit too fond of their own
notoriety. And when the accused comes in,
dressed in faults, in old habits suddenly significant,
a space opens up around that one. It vibrates
like a brass bell after the last note
has rung. Some would say it is the aura
of the devil attending the witch. When one is cast out
into the wilderness, surely the same unassailable
space opens and encloses the pariah.
The people of this village stare with strange eyes
filmed over with an eagerness to see the worst
in a worried old woman or a man who will pay
his debts twice over, for we have suffered here,
we have suffered, and someone has to pay.

Susannah Sheldon Testifies

Susannah was part of a core group of afflicted girls. George Burroughs had been a minister in Salem before moving to Maine.

George Burroughs? His spectre came to torture me.
He grabbed my throat, he yanked my arm—and he's
unnatural strong. His spectre came; it grabbed my throat.
Tortured me. His teeth were gobbed with bloody spit.

His wives, they came in winding sheets and they
did mutter and hiss: they'll wait for him at the hanging tree.
He caused their deaths! His sorcery did. I saw his wives
in winding sheets. And how they muttered, how
they hissed. They'll wait for him at the hanging tree.

I would not sign his Devil's book, no matter how
he tortured me and showed his bloody spit. His wives,
they came in winding sheets and they did hiss.
Unnatural, George Burroughs. He won't be missed.

Thomas and the Wild Thing

I went with Henry West to check his traps.
We heard it before we saw the bloody beast—
a fisher cat snarling and spitting
so fierce even Henry's dog backed up, lay down, and whined.
Henry crushed the fisher cat's head with a stone.
I see it still when I close my eyes at night.

Like the wilderness of that maddened critter,
something coiled up and tight has loosed itself
within those girls: Abigail, Annie, the others.
Wherever it came from, it can't be put right.
Their very teeth seem longer, sharper
and their eyes glitter, as in fever, too bright.

Francis Nurse, After the Hanging

husband of Rebecca Nurse

We waited till nightfall, my sons and I,
then gathered her broken body up.
By candle light my daughters washed her,
combed her, blessed her
with their tender touches.
In the last glimmer of moonlight
we put her to rest in the dark earth
under a pine, near a whispering stream.
A boulder watches over her now.
Patient. Enduring.

~

But I am no stone. A man only.

~

Five weeks it's been. People glance at us
and quickly look away. Friday my son
asked me to go with him to Salem Town
on some sort of business. Sun bright
as an unblinking eye staring down at us.
Gulls wheeling and crying. Salt in the air.
The screech of the gulls won't leave me—
they dive into all my dreams at night.
And by day, all day, I taste salt.
Nothing but salt.

Susannah Accuses the Constable

John Willard was the constable.

Called *us girls* witches. And refused to arrest the evil ones.
Oh, John Willard. Refused to arrest them. Called *us* witches,
and refused. Arrest the evil ones, John Willard. Don't call
us girls witches. He refused to arrest the evil ones.

I saw a ghost lift up its winding sheet, pull a pitchfork
from its wounds. It said *John Willard did this to me.*
Lifted up its winding sheet, a pitchfork in its wounds.
Its winding sheet was lifted up. I saw the ghost.
The pitchfork in its wounds. John Willard did this.

He tried to run away, John Willard did. Captured
forty miles from here. He tried to run, John Willard did.
But he was caught—captured forty miles from here.
Tried to run from his sins, but they captured him.

John Willard's Test

Witches and wizards were thought to be unable to recite the Lord's Prayer correctly.

Our Father, which art in heaven
hollowed be thy name   *Wait! He said HOLLowed.*

Why no, no, that's not what I said. Not—
Our Father, which art in heaven
how—   hallowed by thy name;
thy kingdom come,
thy will be be   be   *Speak up, please.*
done! Thy will be done!
on earth as it is in h-h-h   *He can't say it! The devil's in him!*
earth as in—
and   and our trespasses   *Witch! Wizard! Devil's kin!*
No, wait, please, I'm just,
all of you are so—   *Guilty! He's guilty!*
forgive—
and lead us not
but deliver me, deliver me
from evil   *Evil! He is evil!*
deliver   *Willard, you have failed this test.*
deliver me   *The Lord's Prayer, a simple thing*
                                         for those whose conscience is clear.

forgive us our trespasses!
                                         Take him, then, to the jailhouse.

lead me not   not
                                         You can't run this time, Willard!
                                         Witch! Wizard! Evil!

not   no—
                                         Take him.

Mercy Is Afflicted

Mercy, oh Mercy, your teeth do chatter so—
are you cold?
> *Cold, cold. Should never have told.*

Mercy, oh Mercy, you're rattled and fevered.
Here is broth, can you take some?
> *Nearly done. Black sun. I can take none.*

Mercy, oh Mercy, you're writhing
and choking. What can we do?
> *My throat tattooed. I'm strangled. I'm through.*

Mercy, oh Mercy, we are in darkness here.
What tortures you so?
> *You know, you know. That carrion crow.*

Mercy, oh Mercy, the men have gone with iron chains
to take Mary Esty away.
> *Pole cat, pick axe, jackal, jay.*

Goody Wright Talks with Goody Taber, Who Relates the News to Goody Abbot

Mary Esty? Yes, Mary Esty! Rebecca Nurse's sister? Yes!
Who would have thought it? She seems a gentle soul—
         But she holds darkness, carries evil! You never can tell.

Mary, capable of witchcraft? Magistrate could scarce believe it.
First one and now the other has been found out.
         Rebecca. Mary. It seems I did not know them very well.

Magistrate himself could scarce believe it. Questioned again,
Abigail, then Annie turned flustered, unsure.
         First they accused her; then they admitted doubt.

Well, I'm sorry for those girls. The suffering they've endured…
Maybe, maybe it wasn't her, Annie stammered, wringing her hands.
         Biting her lip she repeated, *Maybe it wasn't her.*

Only Mercy Lewis stayed true to her story, insisting *She's a witch!*
while Abigail stayed silent, and Annie seemed unsure.
         Mary Esty—really a witch? It's hard to tell.

Mary Esty was released. Back to her garden, her baking, her chores.
Mercy stayed true to her story, though, insisting *She's a witch!*
         The Putnams took Mercy home as evening fell.

Mary—could she be a witch? She seemed a gentle soul
pleased to return to her baking, her garden and her chores.
         But something tortured Mercy that very night.

The only one stayed true to her story, the only one said
and said again, *Mary Esty is a witch!* Soon the girl was close to death.
What made Mercy burn with fever? Filled with dread?

Constable returned for Mary. Now she's imprisoned, chained
to the wall. *Seemed* a gentle soul, but she's a witch. You never can tell.
Mercy's stopped convulsing, and once again she's well.

Sarah Cloyce and the Striped Cat

sister of Rebecca Nurse and Mary Esty

Early in the morning
a striped cat trotted out from behind the shed,
a rat dangling from its jaws.

That night I dreamt of it.
Next day I was accused.

September-November, 1692

Thomas Steals Into the Meadow at Midnight

Forty witches at a time, sometimes fifty, maybe more
meet in the meadow just east of our barn
to do black magic. They drink blood!
There in our overgrown pasture they gather.
Abigail claims it's true—true as the scar
that begins on my forehead and slants down, interrupting
my left eyebrow. Worse than the savages what killed a farmer
and his whole family sixty miles from here.

Have you seen them, did you speak, did they hex you,
did they fly, our neighbors, are you sure—
I wanted to know, I wanted to know! But Mother was coming
and Abigail said *Shh, shh, shh.* Flounced away,
all important-like. I hate her sometimes.
But she's not the only one talks that way.
Some that's in prison now said "Devil's Sabbath,"
said "the minister's meadow,"
said "summoned by a trumpet," and more.

Last night the moon was nearly full—the very kind of night
witches like to gather. I'd never once seen them,
or heard them even—why? I wanted to know!
So very late, my father's snores rattling the windows,
I crept out. Took not even a candle. Moonlight enough.
Hid near a clump of pokeberries. Waited. It was lonesome
and shivery. Heard an owl, but couldn't see it.
For a long time then—nothing. I hugged my knees,
put my head down for a minute, maybe more.
Then a low growling or snarling or cursing—something!
and moving fast, twigs snapping, rush of shadows
hard to make out. The moon hid in ragged clouds.

Coming toward me—a sort of yipping—Indians?
Could'a been the Devil himself out there. Ready to grab me.
I ran. Heart thumping, breath rasping, and something chasing.
Fell over something that hit me hard and—
my head was all afire with pain. Dirt in my mouth.

Someone lifting me up.
John Indian shaking me, asking what fool business I was on.
The moon showed itself again and John picked up a hoe
I'd stumbled over, stepped on so the handle whacked my head.
I might've forgot to put it away weeks ago. Or could be
a witch moved it right there, where it would trip me up.

I was bleeding. *It was the witches,* I told him, *they came after me.*
He held up a lantern. He'd been in the barn checking on
the ewe that's likely to drop her lamb any day now—or night.
He'd heard a commotion too. John said it was three coyotes
chasing down some rabbits. But was he sure?
Some witches take the form of hares, he told me,
and do their secret business quiet-like.
Tituba used to tell of such things.

He steered me in, and Father woke. Angry and ghost-like
in his nightshirt. He lit into John and me both, roaring.
Ordered me not to go chasing after witches. He'll have no child
of his a-wandering at night. He'll have no disobedience.
And all like that. Cuffed us both too.
I did not cry. Just looked at the way his hair stuck out all over
and the tip of his nose was white.

Sarah Cloyce, After Her Arrest

Low to the ground and swift
a fox slips into the wood.
        Just so, fear moves, low and quick.

I wear suspicion blind, no holes in the hood,
        the fabric rough and stiff.

Abby Hobbs Is Not the Least Contrite

a young girl whose parents seemed unable to control her

and if I wander the woods at night
   it's because my heart is wild
    it yips and barks and snarls like the coyotes

and if I prefer the pitted moon
to lamp or candlelight
    it's because I swallowed a stone
    at birth that came from the night sky

and if I don't please you
because I will obey neither the church
nor my mother
   why should I care
   I do what pleases me

and if you scold about my dress my hair
the scratches on my skin
    I say my eyes are green
    like the ferns I lie down in
    ferns that smell of rain and fawn and forest

and so I am well-pleased with how I look

and if you would name me Witch
    I do not care
    witches can't be tamed
    I won't be either

Reverend Parris Stays Strong

By God, I have to win this fight. For I am chosen.
>   This is my test.
My failure, if witchcraft prevails, will be complete.
>   No, I will not rest.
People look to me for help. I wonder—have my own sins
>   brought this on?
Witchcraft—it's the Devil's hand! Is it because of what
>   we are within
that it blooms and spreads, like hemlock or hogweed?
>   I do confess

a bit of terror. It started here, in my own home!
>   Are we cursed—or blessed?
Tituba admitted witchcraft and her husband John
>   is sore distressed.
I watch him—don't think he's part of it. I pray to God
>   I am not wrong.
We rent his labor to the tavern; need the money
>   he brings in.
But would arrest him if he did the Devil's work. I'm wary.
>   This is my test.

I long to know the gratitude I'll get if I succeed.
>   Hale has stressed
the weight of this task, and Mather agrees.
>   Now George Burroughs is under arrest.
He ministered here, then left. Misfortune followed him.
>   The man seemed strong
but he gave in to evil. In Maine his village was attacked,
>   burned to the ground.
Now God has chosen me to stand up to Satan.
>   And I will pass this test.

Mary Esty's Last Days

sister of Rebecca Nurse and Sarah Cloyce

I tell myself not to be afraid.
If I meet God, He will know who I am.
If I meet only darkness, it will be like the darkness of sleep
or the forgotten world that cradled me
before birth brought me into the light
and into the confusion of this difficult, beloved world.

I should not cling to the world so much.
Look where it has brought me.
But the fields at sunset when a million
starlings fling themselves across the sky—a dark cloak
turning itself inside out in the wind—there are feelings
I can't explain, and the world has brought me to them.
It is hard to leave a place you've loved.

Life comes from someplace unknowable
and it's glorious for a while.
Summer and winter, bread and salt.
The sky that brings birdsong, raindrops and wind.
Our beautiful world. And then—

Already life has passed through me fifteen times.
That is ordinary enough, but each time
I was filled with awe.

My firstborn, Isaac, gripped his daddy's finger
with his tiny fist. Would not let go. Sarah next,
hiccupped through her infancy, then talked
me into exhaustion from the time she was two.
Hannah and John, blue-eyed Benjamin, serious Joe,

Samuel and Jacob. Josh was a mischief-maker—
some said I loved him best, but how could a mother choose?
Then came sweet Mary, Jeffrey, and the three we buried—
Elizabeth, Eddy, and Lydia, who died in my arms
the day she turned one. They had to pry her from me.
Then Amity—but I was so tired.
Mary was more a mother to her than I was,
and I regret that. We called our youngest
Mary's little shadow. Ah, they will suffer.

Already, I hear, my grandson has run away to some far place,
and plans to change his name, since mine has sullied his.

Jeffrey and Jacob were allowed in
to visit for a moment, to give me a bit of bacon and bread,
squeeze my hand, tell me how Father was holding up.
I saw dark smudges under Jacob's eyes.
I told them to pay no mind to people squawking about witches—
it's just the sound of folk
trying to push a heavy chest against the door.

I told them that. I am trying to believe it.

Martha Corey's Last Hours

a church member in her sixties

first the guttural cries of crows
shadows flapping off

then just the rutted road, the creaking cart
and the rank odor of our bodies

could that be
the evil seeping out

a muttering crowd escorts us
one man's awful smile

the cart stutters
wheels sunk in marshy earth

and we're going
nowhere

my heart flutters
the good Lord must be saying No

to this dirty business
but if that's so, no one pays Him any mind

and it may be a trick of the devil
that what we hear sounds like labor

a mother growling out her babe
but that heaving and grunting

it's men in their shirtsleeves
pushing the wagon out

if this is a birth
it is of our second life, on the other side

we jolt forward
toward the hanging tree

a man on a big black horse
following us, the horse's rolling eye

Abigail Gets Ready to Shout

I never think on my dead parents,
dead sister. That part of my life is blank,
an emptiness. Past. You could say it's full
of all I have not got. Some nights

even the moon is missing, but today
is strange. A pale moon floats like a wafer
in part of the sky, even while the sun
rules the rest. A rooster keeps crowing

though it's nearly noon. He likes to make noise.
I do too. I like to be heard. Like to be looked at.
When girls are too good they're invisible,
done for, as good as dead. A drawing

sticked into the dust, and then rubbed out.
The air is restless today, and the village fills
with horses and footsteps, whispers, shouts.
Bodies rushing by. Crowds hustle to the meeting house

where I'm appearing with Annie and Mercy,
Susannah, and others. We're called *the Afflicted*.
The judges stare over their spectacles at us.
Neighbors too. They wonder just who is a witch,

and who is not. I steady myself, breathe in. I'll let
the terror roll over me, share my torments,
cry out, accuse, accuse, point a trembling finger
at some woman or man who feels righteous—

but is not. I'll have the people look at me,
and listen hard. I'm not afraid to shout. Some girls
may fade like shadows do when the light goes out,
but I—most definitely—will not.

Israel Porter's Inventory

Rebecca Nurse: hanged.

> When we warned her of charges against her,
> she looked at us amazed.
> A kind woman, an old woman
> sick abed, hard of hearing, hardly able to stand.
> And never a cutting word against another.

And her sister Mary Esty.

> From her cell, she petitioned the court
> to please consider—some of the accused
> might be innocent, and therefore unable
> in good conscience to confess.
> Even her jailers bravely stepped forward
> to testify on her pious ways.

The third sister, Sarah Cloyce,

> wife of my good friend Peter, wastes away
> in Boston jail. When Abigail Williams
> named her a witch, poor Sarah fell into a faint
> which was seen as evidence
> of her unnatural ways.

John Willard: hanged

> Should have stayed a farmer. What kind
> of constable refuses to arrest his neighbors?
> Of the accusers, he cried out, *Hang them!*
They're the witches! So they turned on him.

John Proctor: hanged.
        Who worked hard all his life, and prospered.
        True, he was opposed to hiring Reverend Parris.
        And he never believed those finger-pointing girls,
        spoke out against the whole thing.
        Better to have kept his thoughts to himself.

His wife spared—only because she is with child.

Reverend George Burroughs: hanged.
        At his hanging, he recited the Lord's Prayer—
        the words in perfect order, the tone
        sincere. Some decided then and there
        he must be innocent. Cotton Mather rose up
        and warned the crowd not to be fools,
        and spoke of the Devil's deception, how
        it can play out in women and in men.

Martha Corey: hanged.
        A good, church-going woman she was.
        Thought the witchcraft hearings
        were the stuff of nonsense
        until they came for her.

Her husband Giles will be the next to go.

Reverend Hale Worries

The bewitched are strangely powerful; folks hang
       on every word they say
and doubters are accused themselves;
       they're dragged away.
Jails have never been so full; more prisoners
       crowd in day by day.
The bewitched are strangely powerful; folks hang
       on every word they say.
The travails of victims cast their own unholy spell.
       Truth gets lost in our dismay.
Even the righteous can err. But those who speak of doubts
       are made to pay.
The bewitched are strangely powerful; people hang
       on every word they say
while doubters are accused themselves,
       and dragged away.

I've watched some hang; over a hundred
       witches are in jail.
The pious along with the peculiar—prisoners now:
       filthy, frightened, ill.
Could *all* of them be witches? Or
       has justice failed?
I've watched some hang; over a hundred
       suspects are in jail.
Justices say Satan's evil plot has been unveiled.
       Unnerving to hear them speak of it—
their voices tinged with thrill.
       I've watched good people hang; over a hundred
witches are jailed.
       The pious along with the peculiar—prisoners now:
filthy, frightened, ill.

Giles Corey Refuses to Cooperate

a feisty 80-year-old farmer, husband of Martha

Witchcraft, hah!
They accuse me.
Press me to surrender.
            Let them wait.
They mean to hang us all.
Want to see me pleading.
I'll not be their fool.
They twist my words.
I never said
my wife were no witch.
Though I did not like it
when she told me how to pray.
They demand
am I guilty or innocent
as if a word I said
would change their minds.
They mean to hang us all!
            Let them wait.
I won't do it their way.
They press me
to surrender.
Pile rock after rock
after rock.
Demand again
am I guilty or innocent.
I won't do it their way.
            More weight!

Israel Porter Sees a Shameful Thing

An old crank, Giles Corey was,
hard-working and hard-boiled. Cantankerous
stubborn, hot-tempered, mean.
Who had any use for him?
                    But to do THAT
                    to do THAT to anyone—

Well, it's been a hard winter
and an even more difficult spring.
Fears flicker like torch light; sparks of suspicion
catch the wind. Accusations
threaten us all. For who has never sinned?
Who among us does not carry
a stone in his heart?
The weight could suffocate a saint.
                    And saints are few in Salem Village.

When Sheriff Corwin made Corey to lie down, and ordered
stones placed on his chest, Baldwin stepped forward,
put the stone of his own shame on Giles Corey,
and Brown added the rock of his recent failure.
So stone by stone, and rock by rock
we piled our woes on one stubborn man, who was old
and would die soon, this way or another.
                    He refused to cry out.

Near the end when his tongue bulged
out from the cave of his mouth,
Corwin poked it back in with a stick.
We heard the man's ribs crack, saw his skin
turn an awful grayish-purple, but Corey never gave in.
After two long days he died,
                    done in by our sins.

Thomas Remembers Ranger

My bold friend Henry
who tracks game like a savage
and whoops like one too, at times,

obedient to his parents, but wild in the woods—
my good friend Henry,
he cried.

They took his dog away and hanged it
from the tree at Gallows Hill,
just as they did the other witches.

For Mary Warren said that when Ranger looked at her
he held a little growl in the back of his throat
that sounded much like the devil

and gazed at her with unblinking, evil eyes.
His eyes are really golden, like honey
and though Ranger's mostly black,

there's a white circle 'round his left eye.
And a blaze of white on his chest.
Panting and patient, Ranger would lie in the dirt

while we picked burrs and bristles from his fur
and flung away ticks, and scratched him just behind
the ears, while his tail went thump, thump, thump.

They hanged the dog on Saturday.
And Henry cried.

December, 1692 and Later

Goody Abbot, Goody Taber and Goody Wright Consider the Situation

Have you ever seen so many fields neglected? But what
can you expect? People trekking to the jail and back
    to bring to husband, wife, or mother

some beans or bread, a shawl, a lamp, a word. Fields neglected?
What of the children left untended? Like the Proctor
    children I found crying under a willow Tuesday last.

Dirty and hungry, though still well-mannered.
The youngest is only three. The children cried out
    about the sheriff taking all the family's goods,

selling off some cattle—killing the rest. Every bit of food
in their house stolen right out from under them. I gave
    those children bread and apples. But would not let

my own get too close. Best to keep them at a distance.
Scores of families ruined! How can the devil have reached so far?
    And when the sheriff takes their goods? Is that not stealing?

Never mind that. You've heard, have you not, the ones
most lately accused have *NOT* been arrested.
    Not arrested? How is that?

Last week Sarah Hale was pointed out. Sarah Hale—
the reverend's wife! That's made the man think twice
    on how one proves a witch.

Goodwife Hale? The reverend must be shaken.
He knows the girls have suffered, but now he wonders
        have we been mistaken? Well, some do call them liars,

and some say it's all for show. I just don't know. But this
is sure. Lady Phips, the governor's wife, has been accused.
        No! Oh yes, the governor's wife has been accused,

and he will *not* let this go on. Magistrate Saltonstall
left the court. *He* will not go on. He saw no justice
        in the hearings, in families come undone.

And the governor—he's enraged! I don't believe the trials
can continue. In the end, it's hard to know what's justice.
        But the hangings? I pray we've seen the end of those.

What of Reverend Parris? He won't give up. He sees
the devil everywhere. Yes, Parris may continue.
        I find it hard, very hard, to like that man.

He never sees the good in a body, it's true.
And this is also true: behind the closed door of their home
        there may be evidence of evil. But the reverend's wife,

she whispers, *Bring our daughter home now.*
The danger's past. And I believe
        this witchcraft trouble cannot last.

Tituba Watches the Others Go

They've stopped hanging witches. That what they say.
Jailer's wife say everybody tired of the hangings.
I watch as one by one, others are led away.
But Jailer warns me, Don't be in no rush
to see the light of day.

Only a family pays the fees—*then* he lets us go.
Pay for our porridge, straw bedding, chains.
But Master Parris say No, he won't pay.
Unchained, I'm put to sweeping
while I watch the others go.

Echoes

Rye meal and hot piss, baked in ashes—
Enemies conspire against me.
Wintery wind, a potion briefly flying.

I never hurt those children.
We are in darkness here.
Beware of poppets stuck with pins.

Roust the witches out. Fast and pray.
Confess to things I never done?
By the rat's tail, I'll not!

They press me to surrender, rock after rock.
I had my duty and I did it.
They hanged the dog on Saturday.

Some nights, even the moon is missing.
This witchcraft trouble cannot last.
Nightfall, my sons and I gathered her broken body up.

We jolt forward, toward the hanging tree
a man on a big black horse following us,
the horse's rolling eye.

DIRECTORY OF NAMES

Well over 100 people were involved in the witchcraft hysteria in and around Salem Village. Here are some of the individuals mentioned in the book.

THE PARRIS HOUSEHOLD

Reverend Samuel Parris: He secured an appointment in 1689 as minister of Salem Village. He lived in the parsonage with his family.

Elizabeth Parris: The reverend's wife had been one of the beauties of the area, but was likely ill during the witch hunt.

Thomas Parris: He was the oldest Parris child, about twelve or thirteen during the trials.

Betty Parris: She was about nine years old when the witchcraft craze began. Along with her cousin Abigail, she made the first accusations of witchcraft in the Salem area.

Susannah Parris: She was a very young child during the witchcraft proceedings.

Abigail Williams: The orphaned niece of Samuel Parris, she lived with the family in Salem Village throughout the witchcraft hysteria and was one of the most adamant accusers.

Tituba Indian: She was a slave, most likely a Caribbean Indian or mixed-race woman. When Samuel Parris came to Boston from the Barbados, she and her husband came with him. Tituba was the first person to be accused of witchcraft (by Betty and Abigail).

John Indian: He was also a slave, married to Tituba. Often sent out to work at the local tavern or "ordinary."

THE PUTNAM HOUSEHOLD

Thomas Putnam Jr. was an ally of Samuel Parris. Thomas Putnam signed many legal complaints against people accused of witchcraft.

Ann Putnam, wife of Thomas, was an unhappy woman with many complaints.

Annie Putnam (also known as Ann Putnam Jr.) was the oldest child in the family and was among those who accused Tituba, Sarah Good, Sarah Osborne, and others. She was twelve years old when the witchcraft period began.

Mercy Lewis, at age fourteen, had witnessed the murder of her parents at the hands of Indians in Maine. She lived for a while with the family of George Burroughs, and then worked as a servant for the Putnam family.

THE PROCTOR HOUSEHOLD

John Proctor was a very successful farmer and tavern-keeper.

Elizabeth Proctor, John's wife, was pregnant when she was imprisoned as a witch.

Mary Warren, a young woman of about twenty, was an indentured servant in the Proctor household. Early on she joined some of the accusers; then she told the court, "The afflicted persons did but dissemble."

There were numerous children and step-children in the family also, including **Thorndike Proctor.**

THE TOWNE SISTERS

Rebecca Towne Nurse was elderly, ill, and partially deaf when she was accused. Her husband **Francis Nurse** had worked hard, and at last they were leading a prosperous life when she was arrested.

Mary Towne Esty was a highly respected woman and the mother of many children.

Sarah Towne Cloyce, the last of the sisters to be accused, was outspoken and indignant.

OTHERS

Bridget Bishop had been widowed twice and her third marriage was abusive. She was known for her sharp tongue.

George Burroughs had been a minister in Salem Village before moving to Maine. He was known for his great physical strength.

Martha Corey was a church member who was outspoken in her skepticism concerning witchcraft in the community. She was sixty-five years old during the trials.

Giles Corey was an eccentric, eighty-year-old farmer, who had gotten into trouble with the law years before.

George Corwin, son of **Magistrate Jonathan Corwin,** was the sheriff during the witch trials, arresting suspects and presiding over the execution of those condemned for witchcraft.

Sarah Good was one of the first three people arrested. She had been born into a wealthy family but suffered several misfortunes and was penniless by the time of the trials.

Dorcas Good was Sarah's four-year-old daughter.

William Good was the husband of Sarah Good.

Reverend John Hale was a Harvard-educated minister in the nearby town of Beverly. When the fits and outbursts of Samuel Parris' girls bewildered him, he consulted with Hale, who confirmed the diagnosis of the local doctor, that the children were bewitched.

Abby (Abigail) Hobbs was known as an unruly, irreverent girl who often ran wild. Her parents conceded that they had little or no control over her.

Elizabeth Howe was said to be a loving and obedient wife to her blind husband.

Margaret Jones was the first person to be put to death for witchcraft in the Massachusetts Bay Colony, in the 1640's. John Hale witnessed her execution when he was a boy.

Cotton Mather, son of Harvard president and renowned minister **Increase Mather,** used his influence to push for harsh measures against those suspected of witchcraft. He was a prolific writer, many of whose books focused on supernatural events.

Sarah Osborne was one of the first three people arrested. At the time of the trials, she was mostly bed-ridden and possibly beginning to slide into senility or mental illness.

Sir William Phips: A ship's carpenter turned treasure hunter, he was knighted by King James II and became Boston's provost marshal general, and then governor.

Israel Porter was a wealthy land-owner who disapproved of the witchcraft trials and was hostile toward Thomas Putnam and Samuel Parris.

Nathaniel Saltonstall resigned his post as a magistrate in the witchcraft trials after the first hanging, dissatisfied with the way the trials were conducted.

Stephen Sewall's family, who lived in Salem Town (as opposed to the rural outpost known as Salem Village), took in Betty Parris during several months when the witchcraft hysteria had taken over the village. He was a cousin of Samuel Parris. Sewall's brother Samuel was one of the presiding magistrates.

Mary Sibley, a neighbor of the Parris family, suggested to Tituba and John Indian that they make a "witch cake" in order to find out the identity of the witches who were bothering the girls. This was standard folk magic in England, but unacceptable to Reverend Parris.

Mary Walcott was seventeen, the daughter of **Captain Jonathan Walcott**. She was one of the afflicted girls.

John Willard was a deputy constable; his duties including arresting those accused of witchcraft. He could not believe that all of the accused were witches and he began refusing to arrest people.

Goody Abbot, Goody Taber, Goody Wright, Joseph Leech, and **Henry West** are fictional characters.

Note: Spellings of names in historical records vary.

ABOUT THE AUTHOR

Ginny Lowe Connors is the author of two previous poetry collections: *The Unparalleled Beauty of a Crooked Line* and *Barbarians in the Kitchen*, as well as a chapbook, *Under the Porch,* winner of the Sunken Garden Poetry Prize. In addition, she has edited several anthologies. Connors, who earned an MFA in poetry from Vermont College of Fine Arts, has served as the poet laureate of her town, West Hartford, Connecticut, where she worked as an English teacher for many years. She also runs a small poetry press, Grayson Books. You can find out more about her poetry by visiting her website: www.ginnyloweconnors.com.

This book has been set in Garamond, a typeface created by Claude Garamond in the first part of the Sixteenth Century. He based his font on types cut by Francesco Griffo for Venetian printer Aldus Manutius in 1495. Garamond created a typeface with an unprecedented degree of balance and elegance, for centuries standing as the pinnacle of beauty and practicality in type-founding. Italics for the Garamond font are based on those cut by Robert Granjon (1513–1589).

To order additional copies of this book
or other Antrim House titles, contact the publisher at

Antrim House
21 Goodrich Rd., Simsbury, CT 06070
www.antrimhousebooks.com
860.217.0023, AntrimHouse@comcast.net.

·

On the house website
in addition to information on books
you will find excerpts, upcoming events, and
a "seminar room" featuring supplemental biography,
notes, images, poems, reviews, and
writing suggestions.